Global Change Strategic Science Planning Team

Public Review Draft--USGS Global Change Science Strategy: A Framework for Understanding and Responding to Climate and Land-Use Change

By Virginia R. Burkett, Ione L. Taylor, Jayne Belnap, Thomas M. Cronin, Michael D. Dettinger, Eldrich L. Frazier, John W. Haines, David A. Kirtland, Thomas R. Loveland, Paul C.D. Milly, Robin O'Malley, and Robert S. Thompson

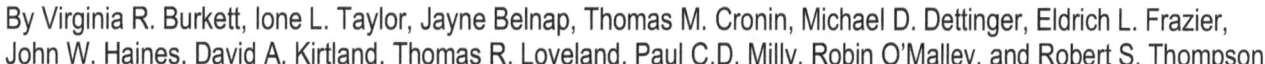

Open-File Report 2011–1033

U.S. Department of the Interior
U.S. Geological Survey

U.S. Department of the Interior
KEN SALAZAR, Secretary

U.S. Geological Survey
Marcia K. McNutt, Director

U.S. Geological Survey, Reston, Virginia: 2011

For product and ordering information:
World Wide Web: *http://www.usgs.gov/pubprod*
Telephone: 1–888–ASK–USGS

For more information on the USGS—the Federal source for science about the Earth,
its natural and living resources, natural hazards, and the environment:
World Wide Web: *http://www.usgs.gov*
Telephone: 1–888–ASK–USGS

Suggested citation:
Burkett, V.R. and others, 2011, Public review draft; USGS global change science strategy: A framework for understanding and responding to climate and land-use change, U.S. Geological Survey Open-File Report 2011–1033, 32 p., at *http://pubs.usgs.gov/of/2011/1033.*

Contents

Figures

USGS Global Change Science Strategy: A Framework for Understanding and Responding to Climate and Land-Use Change

By Virginia R. Burkett,[1] Ione L. Taylor,[1] Jayne Belnap,[2] Thomas M. Cronin,[2] Michael D. Dettinger,[2] Eldrich L. Frazier,[2] John W. Haines,[2] David A. Kirtland,[2] Thomas R. Loveland,[2] Paul C.D. Milly,[2] Robin O'Malley,[2] and Robert S. Thompson[2]

About this Report

This U.S. Geological Survey (USGS) Global Change Science Strategy expands on the Climate Variability and Change science component of the USGS 2007 Science Strategy, "Facing Tomorrow's Challenges: USGS Science in the Coming Decade" (U.S. Geological Survey, 2007). Here we embrace the broad definition of global change provided in the U.S. Global Change Research Act of 1990 (Public Law 101-606,104 Stat. 3096-3104)—"Changes in the global environment (including alterations in climate, land productivity, oceans or other water resources, atmospheric chemistry, and ecological systems) that may alter the capacity of the Earth to sustain life"—with a focus on climate and land-use change.

There are three major characteristics of this science strategy. First, it addresses the science required to broadly inform global change policy, while emphasizing the needs of natural-resource managers and reflecting the role of the USGS as the science provider for the Department of the Interior and other resource-management agencies. Second, the strategy identifies core competencies, noting 10 critical capabilities and strengths the USGS uses to address key problem areas. We highlight those areas in which the USGS is a science leader, recognizing the strong partnerships and effective collaboration that are essential to address complex global environmental challenges. Third, it uses a query-based approach listing key research questions that need to be addressed to create an agenda for hypothesis-driven global change science organized under six strategic goals. Overall, the strategy starts from where we are, provides a vision for where we want to go, and then describes high-priority strategic actions, including outcomes, products, and partnerships that can get us there.

Global change science is a well-defined research field with strong linkages to the ecosystems, water, energy and minerals, natural hazards, and environmental health components of the USGS Science Strategy (2007). When science strategies that cover these other components are developed, coordinated implementation will be necessary to achieve Bureau-level synergies and optimize capabilities and expertise.

In October 2010, USGS realigned its management and budget structure to implement its 2007 Science Strategy. The new organizational structure, in which "Global Change" is one of seven key mission areas, lends itself to the advancement of the established six strategic goals. USGS Global

---

[1] Co-chair, Global Change Strategic Science Planning Team.
[2] Team member, Global Change Strategic Science Planning Team.

change science is formally represented by the "Climate and Land Use Change" Mission Area in the FY 2012 budget (USGS, 2011).

This plan was developed by the USGS Global Change Science Strategy Planning Team (SSPT) appointed by the USGS Director on March 4, 2010 and charged with developing a Global Change Science Strategy for the coming decade (McNutt, 2010). USGS managers and science staff are the main audience for this science strategy. This document is also intended to serve as the foundation for consistent USGS collaboration and communication with partners and stakeholders.

Executive Summary

The U.S. Geological Survey (USGS), a nonregulatory Federal science agency with national scope and responsibilities, is uniquely positioned to serve the Nation's needs in understanding and responding to global change, which includes changes in climate; sea level; land use and land cover; ecosystems; and the global water, carbon, and nitrogen cycles. Global change is among the most challenging and formidable issues confronting our Nation and society. Scientists agree that global environmental changes during this century will have far-reaching societal implications [Intergovernmental Panel on Climate Change (IPCC), 2007; USGCRP, 2009]. In the face of these complex challenges, the Nation can benefit greatly by using natural science information in decisionmaking.

Over the past 20 years, the USGS Global Change Program has made significant scientific contributions to understanding the interactive living and nonliving components of the Earth system. USGS natural science activities have led to fundamental advances in observing and understanding climate and land-cover change and the impact these changes have on ecosystems, natural-resource availability, and societal sustainability. Most of these major advances were pursued in partnership with others. The inherent value of partnerships—among USGS mission areas and with other U.S. Global Change Research Program (USGCRP) agencies and natural-resource managers—is emphasized in all aspects of planning and implementation of this USGS Global Change Science Strategy for the coming decade.

Over the next 10 years, the USGS will make substantial contributions to understanding how Earth systems interact, respond to, and cause global change. The USGS will work with science partners, decisionmakers, and resource managers at local to international levels to improve understanding of past and present change; develop relevant forecasts; and identify those lands, resources, and communities most vulnerable to global change processes. Science will play an essential role in helping communities and land and resource managers understand local to global implications, anticipate effects, prepare for changes, and reduce the risks of decisionmaking in a changing environment. USGS partners and stakeholders will benefit from the data, predictive models, and decision-support products and services resulting from the implementation of this strategy.

This Global Change Science Strategy recognizes core USGS strengths and applies them to address key societal problems. It defines six programmatic goals for USGS global change science over the short term (1–5 years) and the longer term (5–10 years). Progress towards these six goals will improve understanding of:

1. Rates, causes, and impacts of past global changes.
2. The global carbon cycle.
3. Land-use and land-cover change rates, causes, and consequences.
4. Droughts, floods, and water availability under changing land use and climate.

5. Coastal response to sea-level rise, climatic hazards, and human development.

6. Biological responses to global change.

Next, we discuss the central role of monitoring in accordance with the USGS Science Strategy recommendation that global change research should rely on existing "decades of observational data and long-term records to interpret consequences of climate variability and change to the Nation's biological populations, ecosystems, and land and water resources" (2007, p. 19). Finally, we address the need for a comprehensive and sustained communications strategy.

Introduction

Science for a Changing World

Since it was created by Congress in 1879, the U.S. Geological Survey (USGS) has evolved from an organization charged with inventorying the Nation's public lands and natural resources to an accomplished research institution with broad scientific objectives. Its central mission in the 21st Century is "Science for a Changing World," in recognition of the role that science and scientists can play in monitoring, understanding, and forecasting global environmental change and in informing mitigation and adaptation strategies. This document presents a focused vision and strategy to guide global change science within the USGS in both the short (1–5 years) and the longer (5–10 years) term. It takes into account anticipated national and Department of the Interior needs and the current capabilities and core strengths of the USGS.

Global change refers to changes in the global environment that may alter the Earth's capacity to sustain life and human endeavor (U.S. Global Change Research Act, 1990). This includes alterations in climate, atmospheric chemistry, oceans or other water resources, the land surface and its biological productivity, and ecological systems, including the goods and services they provide. Figure 1 depicts key physical drivers of global change and their interaction with human populations and ecosystems. Collectively, global change and its effects are among the most challenging and formidable issues confronting our Nation and society, and solutions call for a deep appreciation of the complex relations among Earth systems and human activities.

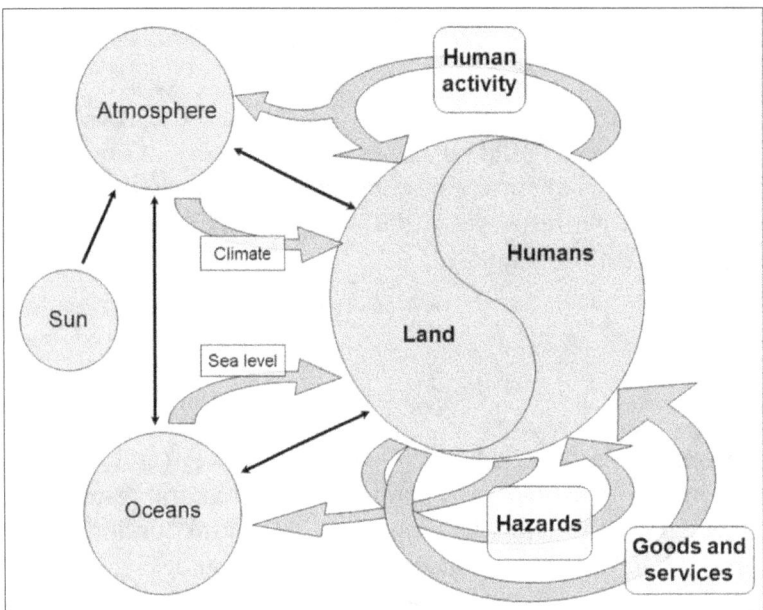

Figure 1. A simplified, land- and human-centered view of the complex Earth system. People affect the Earth system largely through activities on the land surface. In turn, through myriad natural processes, people are affected by Earth-system changes largely through the impacts of those changes on land—where people live.

The USGS has the breadth and ability to interpret these relations and provide high-quality, unbiased science to support decisionmaking. Our multidisciplinary scientific expertise spans the natural sciences and provides a unique understanding of Earth-system science. The USGS has the institutional capacity to provide integrated information, natural process understanding, predictive scenarios, and the technological tools needed to manage the Nation's mineral, energy, water, land, and living resources.

This science strategy presents specific goals and objectives for the Bureau to achieve the following vision for the USGS Global Change Science Program:

USGS scientists will use long-term observational records and process-oriented research to interpret causes and consequences of global change; provide expert, interdisciplinary advice on risks to infrastructure, human safety, and environment; and conduct regional and national assessments that are widely used by policymakers, natural-resource managers, and the public.

Envisioning the Science Basis for Resource Management and Decisionmaking

The Department of the Interior (Interior) manages approximately 20 percent of the land in the United States and adjacent coastal waters. Interior management and stewardship responsibilities include migratory, threatened, and endangered species; National Parks, Wildlife Refuges, Monuments, and other public lands; water resources in the West; Native American trust resources; and the U.S. freely associated States and insular territories. Many sections of this document refer to the needs of decisionmakers in Interior agencies and others under the stewardship umbrella of Interior.

In addition to responding to the science needs of the Interior Bureaus, this science strategy addresses needs of natural-resource managers at local, regional, State, and Federal levels. The USGS also contributes to national and international scientific activities that inform societies about the nature and impact of global change, including participation in climate-change assessments by the U.S. Global Change Research Program (USGCRP) and the Intergovernmental Panel on Climate Change (IPCC).

In the coming decades, resource managers in the United States and other nations will be challenged to make management and policy-level decisions that reduce or forestall adverse consequences, while increasing the potential benefits associated with a changing global environment. Over the 10-year period covered by this science strategy, the USGS can make substantial contributions to understanding how Earth systems interact, respond to, and cause global change as well as how we can restore resilience to impacted systems. Increased understanding of global change impacts, through implementation of a coherent science plan, can provide policymakers, elected officials, and resource managers with sound scientific information to make informed decisions on how best to manage lands, resources, and communities under changing conditions.

This Global Change Science Strategy presents strategic science goals, monitoring objectives, and communication strategies the USGS can implement to achieve the vision described in this report. The goals are integrative and crosscutting, and their success depends on the USGS's ability to recruit, retain, and nurture a workforce with the appropriate mix of skills and expertise.

Core Strengths, Partnerships, and Science Integration

Through its scientific contributions, the USGS has improved understanding of the interactive components of the Earth's terrestrial systems. The USGS occupies a unique position in the global change science community with its long-term, process-based research; observational networks; and extensive databases encompassing the fields of geology, hydrology, climate history, land-use and land-cover change, ecosystem science, and carbon and nutrient cycles. Documenting, understanding, and predicting environmental and natural-resource change at a national scale have been the core of USGS research since it was established 131 years ago. In recent years, USGS scientists have addressed questions about the causes and effects of these changes from local to global scales.

With data from its long-term observational networks and extensive databases; analysis and modeling capabilities; and diverse scientific expertise, the USGS provides broad perspectives needed to expand understanding of past, current, and future global changes and their effects on the Nation's resources and economy. The USGS works with local, State, Federal, nongovernmental, private, and tribal partners to understand past climate variability and deliver credible future scenarios of global-change effects on land, water, and ecological and biological resources. Integrative systems modeling enables USGS scientists to test current understanding of how systems respond to global changes and project those responses forward to support iterative adaptive management, an essential component of environmental and natural-resource stewardship. Figure 2 (see next page) highlights examples of core USGS strengths that are central to the way the USGS and its employees conduct global change science. The following examples demonstrate how these core strengths have been applied by USGS scientists to deliver timely, relevant, and quality science:

- Landsat satellite imagery
  - Management and delivery of the world's longest continuously acquired collection of space-based land remote-sensing data.
  - National assessment of 30 years of U.S. land-use and land-cover change.
- Lead authorship on reports critical to informing public policy
  - U.S. national assessments of climate change and IPCC assessment reports
  - Coordination of and contribution to USGCRP synthesis and assessment products on the following:
    - Abrupt climate change.
    - Climate change and the Arctic and high latitudes.
    - Thresholds of climate change and ecosystems.
    - State of the carbon cycle.
    - Sea-level rise.
- Global and regional future projections of river runoff due to climate change.
- Developed methodologies for assessing carbon sequestration and storage in geologic formations and terrestrial ecosystems.
  - Detection of ongoing climatic trends and impacts, such as
    - Seasonally earlier peak streamflow in the U.S. northeast and west.
    - Seasonally earlier arrival of spring migrant birds.
    - Retreating glaciers in Alaska and the Cascades and Rocky Mountains.
    - Declining permafrost in Alaska.
- Global reconstruction and model simulations of past global warmth and impacts.
- Arctic-wide assessment of polar bear and sea-ice habitat vulnerability to future climate change.
- Sea-level rise vulnerability maps for all U.S. coastal regions and coastal National Parks.

Many of these exemplary products were developed in collaboration with external partners or through internal collaborations that were supported by two or more of the science disciplines (that is, Biology, Geography, Geology, and Water) represented in the USGS structure prior to its realignment in 2010. The reorganization of USGS programs around the six new "mission areas," including global change, emphasizes the continuing importance of fostering collaboration that brings together the necessary core strengths from across the Bureau to understand the processes that collectively affect natural systems.

Figure 2. Integrated Science for Global Change

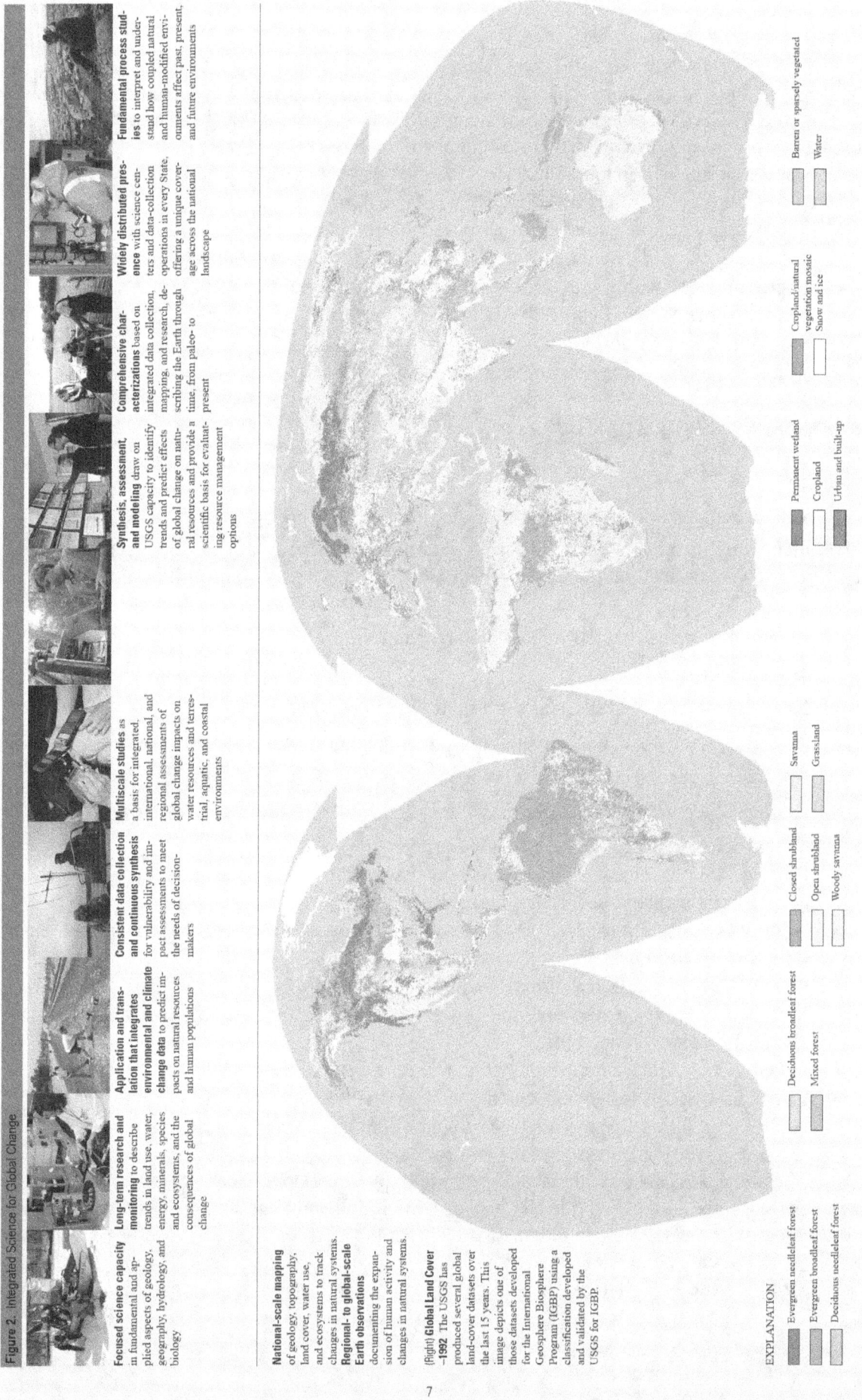

Focused science capacity in fundamental and applied aspects of geology, geography, hydrology, and biology

Long-term research and monitoring to describe trends in land use, water, energy, minerals, species and ecosystems, and the consequences of global change

Application and translation that integrates environmental and climate change data to predict impacts on natural resources and human populations

Consistent data collection and continuous synthesis for vulnerability and impact assessments to meet the needs of decision-makers

Multiscale studies as a basis for integrated, international, national, and regional assessments of global changes impacts on water resources and terrestrial, aquatic, and coastal environments

Synthesis, assessment, and modeling draw on USGS capacity to identify trends and predict effects of global change on natural resources and provide a scientific basis for evaluating resource management options

Comprehensive characterizations based on integrated data collection, mapping, and research, describing the Earth through time, from paleo- to present

Widely distributed presence with science centers and data-collection operations in every State, offering a unique coverage across the national landscape

Fundamental process studies to interpret and understand how coupled natural and human-modified environments affect past, present, and future environments

National-scale mapping of geology, topography, land cover, water use, and ecosystems to track changes in natural systems. **Regional- to global-scale Earth observations** documenting the expansion of human activity and changes in natural systems.

(Right) **Global Land Cover –1992** The USGS has produced several global land-cover datasets over the last 15 years. This image depicts one of those datasets developed for the International Geosphere Biosphere Program (IGBP) using a classification developed and validated by the USGS for IGBP.

EXPLANATION

Evergreen needleleaf forest

Evergreen broadleaf forest

Deciduous needleleaf forest

Deciduous broadleaf forest

Mixed forest

Closed shrubland

Open shrubland

Woody savanna

Savanna

Grassland

Permanent wetland

Cropland

Urban and built-up

Cropland/natural vegetation mosaic

Snow and ice

Barren or sparsely vegetated

Water

The USGS provides its integrated science products within the context of overall Federal efforts to understand and address global change. The USGCRP, comprised of 13 Federal science agencies, including the USGS, is charged with implementing the U.S. Global Change Research Act of 1990. As a multiagency program, USGCRP harnesses the unique approaches and missions of its participating agencies to encourage research that leads to expanded and new results. The USGS contributes directly to strategic priorities established by USGCRP (USGCRP, in press):

- Improving our knowledge of Earth's past and present climate variability and change.
- Improving our understanding of natural and human forces of climate change.
- Improving our capability to model and predict future conditions and impacts.
- Assessing the Nation's vulnerability to current and anticipated impacts of climate change.
- Providing climate information and decision-support tools.
- Climate-change communication and education.

Science Goals and Objectives

Overview

This global change science strategy recognizes core USGS strengths and applies them to address key problems. In this section, we define six programmatic goals for USGS global change science over the short term (1–5 years) and the longer term (5–10 years). The six goals will improve understanding of:

1. Rates, causes, and impacts of past global changes.
2. The global carbon cycle.
3. Land-use and land-cover change rates, causes, and consequences.
4. Droughts, floods, and water availability under changing land use and climate.
7. Coastal response to sea-level rise, climatic hazards, and human development; and
8. Biological responses to global change.

Each goal was selected based on the following criteria:
- Employs integrated scientific research and assessment to fill substantial knowledge gaps about national climate, land-use, ecosystem, and energy priorities.
- Addresses topics critical for managing natural resources and the environment, with tangible effects on environmental goods, services, and risks.
- Uses USGS core capacity, disciplinary strengths, integrative capacities, and long-term databases.
- Invests in comprehensive, integrated observation and monitoring to understand local to global change processes and conditions.
- Leverages or expands partnerships that advance the science goal.
- Builds on USGS's leadership role in, and links with science priorities of, the USGCRP.
- Addresses topics critical to the Department of the Interior for sustainably managing natural resources, wildlife habitat, and the environment.

These six goals are not intended to be distinct, nonoverlapping categories for USGS global-change projects, nor do they include all areas of USGS global change science. Rather, they highlight priority areas where resources should be directed over the next 5 to 10 years. Many topical research needs, which may not be explicitly stated in these six goals, are nonetheless essential for the Global Change program success. Actions recommended to achieve these six strategic goals will either depend on or influence products and outcomes from the other goals—a process consistent with interactions and feedbacks among global change drivers and impacts shown in figure 3.

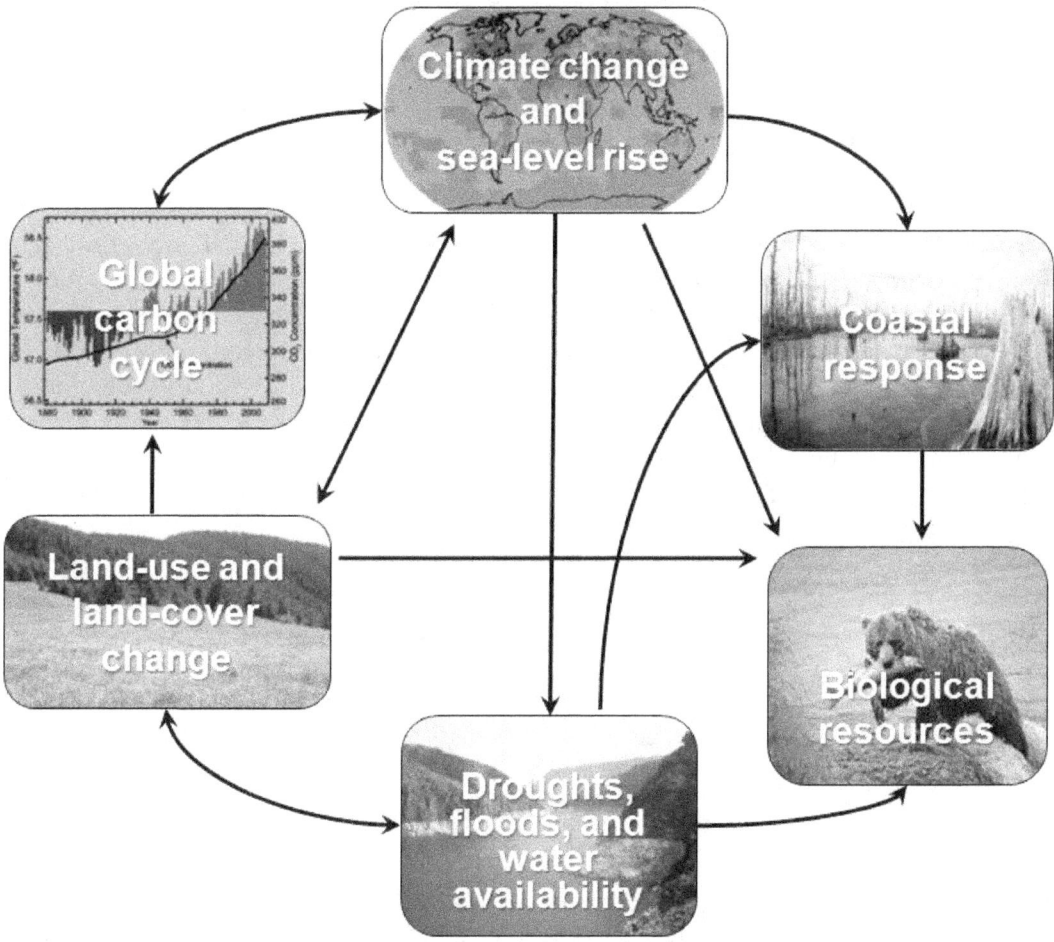

Figure 3.   Figure illustrating connectivity among the six fundamental science goals for the USGS Global Change Program.

The six goals and research needs described in this section reflect an integrated approach to USGS global change research. This approach requires integrating scientific data from the geological record, hydrological processes, land-use history, and ecological expertise to understand natural and anthropogenic changes and their impacts. It is important to note that some physical environments and ecosystems are considered more vulnerable to global change because they are crossing thresholds of sustainability faster than other environments or regions. Crossing a threshold of sustainability means an ecosystem has experienced such a degree or rate of change that it is no longer resilient enough to return to its previous productive state. In addition to concentrating on the most sensitive and vulnerable regions and systems, the USGS must focus its resources on systems of concern to Interior's resource management agencies. Many strategic actions described in the following sections will address highly vulnerable or high-priority Interior-managed landscapes, such as high-latitude and high-elevation environments; drylands, wetlands, and aquatic systems; and resource development lands. Individual species responses are also of great concern to many USGS partners. The USGS will build on a strong capacity and long history of understanding species' response to environmental change as it implements a plan for its new National Climate Change and Wildlife Science Center.

The six scientific goals indicated by boxes in figure 3 are necessarily interconnected, both programmatically and scientifically. The carbon cycle, for example, interacts directly with changes in climate and land use, which in turn affect and are affected by species response and hydrology. Monitoring, modeling, research, and decisionmaking relating to any of these goals will need to be coordinated with all the others; therefore, the science goals are scientific concentrations in a broader continuum of efforts rather than strictly separate activities. Similarly, the global change theme cannot be fully separated from the other science mission areas within the USGS, as suggested in figure 4. Global change is expected to alter the conditions and occurrence of hazards and to challenge ecosystems and natural-resource systems (including water resources) and may depend on carbon sequestration and energy strategies that will be informed by USGS energy and minerals science and assessments. Consequently, this global change science strategy and, specifically, the six goals described in this section will need to draw upon and be coordinated with the science conducted under the other USGS mission areas, while also contributing to those other themes where applicable. Data and information, for example, developed under the Climate and Land-Use Change Mission Area will be integrated with data and information from all the other themes to form a broad and seamless earth sciences whole.

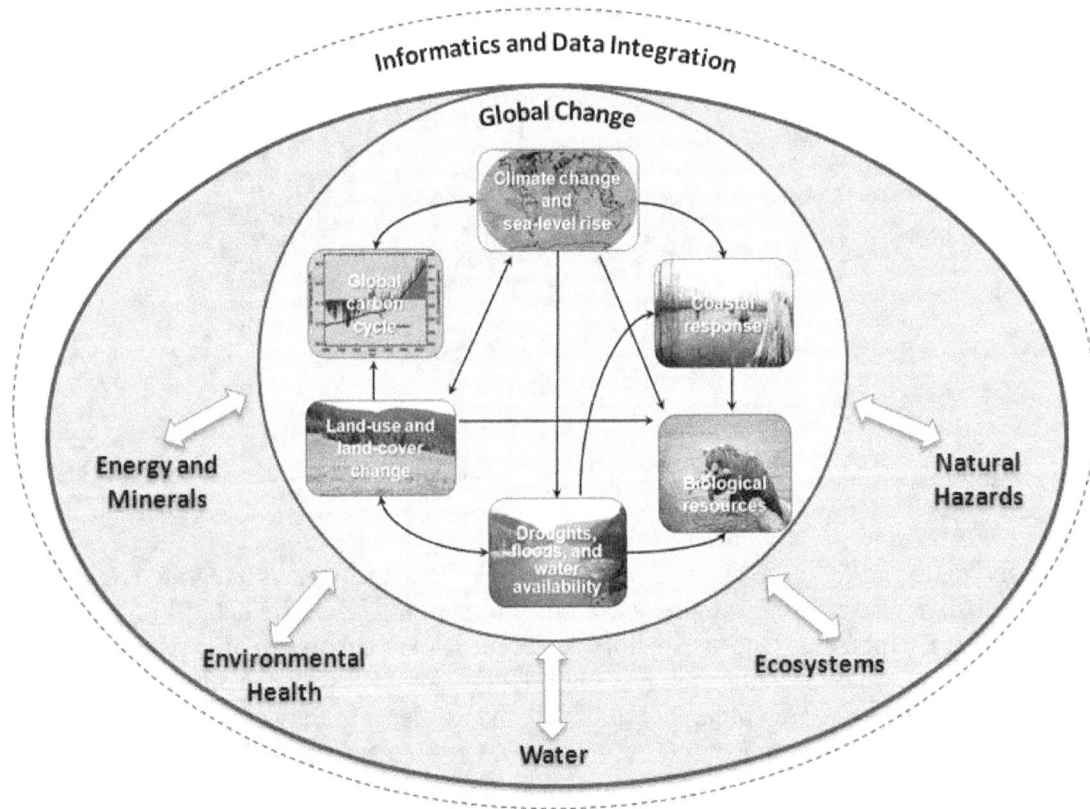

Figure 4.   Relationships among global change and the six other USGS mission areas.

Goals for USGS Global Change Science

The six high-priority goals are developed in more detail below, starting with a statement summarizing the specific societal issues and challenges faced or anticipated. A vision statement and a series of the key scientific research questions pertinent to the goal follow. Finally, a set of short-term and longer term strategic actions are described that, if implemented, will advance USGS science from its current state toward the desired future state articulated in the vision statement.

Goal 1. Improve understanding of past global changes in support of policy and management decisions

Since its inception in 1879, the USGS has conducted research regarding what is today called global change. The Bureau has sought to understand variability and changes in land and water resources, geologic processes, and other aspects of the Earth system. Its scientists have carried out studies of past and ongoing changes in diverse environments throughout the United States and across the globe. These investigations were begun long before the current focus on greenhouse effects because global change did not begin with climatic and environmental changes associated with the industrial revolution. On the contrary, over hundreds of millions of years the Earth system of interacting geologic, atmospheric, hydrologic, and biologic processes has undergone continual variations and changes. These changes have been caused by external forcings such as the Milankovitch cycles of the Earth's orbit, by the internal dynamics of the highly complex Earth system with its many interacting components that can produce phenomena, such as the El Niño-Southern Oscillation variations of the tropical Pacific, and by disturbances to the system, such as those caused by asteroid impacts and human actions. Some of these changes were slow, others abrupt; some were periodic, while others had irregular and surprising amplitudes or rates. The latter may have been related to climatic or environmental thresholds that, when exceeded, resulted in cascading responses.

Nonlinear responses and abrupt changes are two particularly poorly understood phenomena that may come to be critically important in the near-term global changes we now face. Both of these phenomena depend on poorly understood and predicted feedbacks in the Earth system. The instrumental record is too short to reveal the range of variability in climatic and environmental changes or to identify the most dangerous of the potential triggers and thresholds. It is of vital importance to the future of our planet that we understand better how the Earth system functions and how it responds to forcings and perturbations beyond those of the past few decades. Much of the information needed for this understanding lies in the more distant past variations of the Earth system. The Earth has had warmer and colder climates in the past than it does today, large fluctuations in levels of atmospheric carbon dioxide, and many associated changes in ecosystems and other aspects of the surficial environment. Therefore, studies of past conditions and changes provide a basis for properly assessing potential ranges and uncertainties of impacts from various levels of human-induced climate change. The studies also provide the basis for constructing and validating conceptual and computer models of the workings of, and interactions among, key components of the Earth system, providing a foundation for efforts to assess and predict vulnerabilities of specific landscapes, ecosystems, and natural resources to global changes.

Today the USGS has strong and developing capabilities in many fields required to document and understand past global changes, including geology, paleontology, paleohydrology, geochemistry, numerical analysis, and modeling. The Bureau's breadth of scientific expertise will be applied to characterize and understand past global changes from the last century back through millions of years of Earth's history. Insights from historical, paleoenvironmental, and paleoclimatic studies will be increasingly used to support management and policy decisions in the management of water and other natural resources and in national and international planning for the potential consequences of future global changes. The success of USGS research on past global change will to a large degree depend on meaningful linkages with other USGS mission areas and outside collaborators, including the National Oceanic and Atmospheric Administration (NOAA), the National Science Foundation (NSF), other Interior agencies and Federal bureaus, academic researchers, and international scientific organizations.

Vision Statement

The USGS will elucidate past global changes, including characteristics of past climate states and variability; past rates of change; and interactions among climatic, hydrologic, biologic, geologic, and human-induced processes. This information will provide a framework for understanding ongoing and projected climatic and environmental changes and will contribute to the scientific basis for management and policy decisions.

Major Questions

- What were the patterns of change and variability in climate, greenhouse gases, and earth-surface environments over timescales ranging from the past few decades to millions of years?
- What were the causes, durations, levels of greenhouse gases and ocean acidification, and environmental characteristics of past warm climate episodes, such as the Pliocene, Last Interglacial, and Holocene thermal maximum?
- How do ongoing and projected changes in climate, water resources, ecosystems, and the surficial environment compare with past climatic shifts and degrees of variability reconstructed for the past hundreds to thousands of years?
- How rapid and widespread have past global changes been, and were there thresholds that, when crossed, led to unexpected or nonlinear responses in climate, hydrology, ecosystems, or other aspects of the Earth system?
- What can global changes of the past reveal about the vulnerabilities of specific ecosystems, natural resources, or landscapes to particular changes in climate, atmospheric chemistry, or other components of the Earth system? How can this information be used in decision support for management?
- How did humans modify the environment and climate prior to and since the industrial revolution? How have forest clearances, water storage and irrigation systems, and other economic activities affected ecosystems, landscapes, and natural resources?
- How can the acquisition, synthesis, and analysis of historical records and paleodata contribute to the scientific basis of management and policy decisions? How can communication with users be improved?

Strategic Actions and Products

Short term (1–5 years)

- Establish or improve methods for reconstructing and dating changes in mean conditions (and variability around these means) of climatic parameters, land-surface conditions, hydrology, marine environments, and other important facets of past global change.
- Create a national synthesis of currently available data on past climatic and environmental changes and variability, particularly for vulnerable natural resources, lands, and marine environments managed by the Federal Government.
- Improve understanding of past interactions among key components of the Earth system, such as climate, hydrology, and earth-surface processes.

- Investigate the amplitudes, spatial extents, and causes of past abrupt global changes and nonlinear responses to external forcing in climate, land surface, hydrology, and ecosystems.
- Expand the participation of the USGS in national efforts, such as NOAA's National Geophysical Data Center, and international activities, such as IPCC assessments, to use paleodata to evaluate the potential consequences of future global change and to assess the abilities of models to simulate past changes and their effects.

Longer term (5–10 years)

- Conduct focused studies on the climatic and environmental characteristics of past periods of warmer global climates and of higher-than-present levels of greenhouse gases and identify the causes of these episodes and of their terminations.
- Contribute insights from the past in the construction and validation of Earth system models in collaboration with other research groups.
- Assess patterns of climatic and environmental variability from the recent past to the past few millions of years to provide a framework for understanding potential future global change.
- Work with natural-resource managers and policymakers to determine information needs and to enhance communication of paleoperspectives on ongoing and potential future global change.
- Document how species and ecosystems have adapted to past global change and use this information to evaluate the vulnerability of these natural resources to potential future changes.

Goal 2. Improve understanding and prediction of the global carbon cycle

Climate and energy policies are inextricably linked to the global carbon cycle through atmospheric carbon dioxide (CO_2). Studies of the global carbon cycle are critical to understanding potential effects of CO_2 emissions from burning fossil fuels and changing land use. These studies will also inform potential mitigation options for sequestration and storage in Earth systems. The future course of atmospheric CO_2 and global climate will be determined by complex interactions between human activities and carbon-cycle processes that exchange CO_2 with the oceans and terrestrial systems. Policy decisions require information about potential effectiveness of emission reductions and other mitigation activities, as well as the extent to which these measures might be offset by response of the global carbon cycle to climate and land-use change. The USGS will provide scientific information essential for these decisions in support of sound national policies.

Today's elevated atmospheric CO_2 concentrations are unprecedented in the last 3 million years. Policy and legislative decisions about energy policy, resource management, and carbon accounting must be based on many factors, including scientific and nonscientific considerations. Scientific information about the global carbon cycle is essential to anticipate potential impacts on atmospheric CO_2 on society, species, and ecosystems. USGS research on the carbon cycle will focus on interactions among climate change, land-use change, atmospheric CO_2, and other components of the carbon cycle. The most important topics will include improved carbon-cycle modeling; reconstruction of past periods of rising and high CO_2 and global warming; investigation of ocean acidification impacts on marine ecosystems; methane release from permafrost, wetlands, and marine gas hydrates; and relations between land use and carbon cycling.

In addition to these key research activities, USGS carbon cycle expertise will help develop methodologies for a national comprehensive assessment of carbon sequestration resources as mandated by the Energy Independence and Security Act of 2007. The USGS is developing a methodology for assessing ecological carbon stocks, carbon sequestration, and greenhouse gas fluxes. This methodology includes mapping and modeling land-use and land-cover changes, ecosystem disturbances, carbon stocks and potential sequestration, methane and nitrous oxide fluxes, cost benefit analyses, and improved statistical verification methods. The USGS is also developing a probabilistic methodology for evaluating geologic carbon dioxide storage. This methodology estimates pore volume of potential storage formations across a range of uncertainty levels based on information about geologic, geochemical, and hydrologic processes. Following these near-term, national-scale assessments of sequestration capacities, new observational capabilities and research efforts will be needed to more precisely characterize geochemical, hydrologic, and rock mechanical issues raised at specific sequestration sites.

The National Research Council (NRC) report, "Global Environmental Change: Research Pathways for the Next Decade," specifically emphasized the need for a comprehensive carbon cycle research strategy (NRC, 1999). In response, the Carbon and Climate Working Group of USGCRP wrote, "A U.S. Carbon Cycle Science Plan" (Sarmiento and Wofsy, 1999) to establish the U.S. Carbon Cycle Science Program. The USGS collaborates with nine other agencies through this program to clarify the changes, magnitudes, and distributions of carbon sources and sinks; the fluxes between the major terrestrial, oceanic, and atmospheric carbon reservoirs; and the underlying mechanisms involved, including humans, fossil fuel emissions, land use, and climate.

Vision Statement

The USGS will provide scientific information that informs national climate, energy, and land-management policy decisions affecting atmospheric CO_2 concentrations.

Major Questions

- What are the effects of past, present, and potential future human activities on carbon cycling and atmospheric concentrations of CO_2, methane, and other greenhouse gases?
- What is the potential for increasing and sustaining storage of carbon in U.S. geological and ecological systems?
- What are the biological, hydrological, geophysical, and geochemical processes that determine impacts of climate and land-use change on the carbon cycle?
- What do past interactions among the global carbon cycle, atmospheric CO_2, atmospheric methane, and climate tell us about potential future interactions?
- What are the most important amplifying and dampening carbon-cycle feedbacks that will result from rising greenhouse gas concentrations?
- How is the carbon cycle affected by changes in biogeochemical cycling of water, energy, sediments, and nutrients?
- What underlying geologic and geomorphic parameters most significantly impact the magnitude, capacity, and storage time of CO2 sequestration?

Strategic Actions and Products:

Short term (1–5 years)

- Develop assessment methodologies for estimating potential carbon sequestration (volume capacity and distribution) and carbon storage vulnerability in geological and ecological systems.
- Conduct fundamental research that complements the work performed by the Department of Energy and others on the geologic, hydrologic, and geochemical processes in the subsurface that

control and (or) result from the injection of large quantities of liquid carbon dioxide into oil and gas reservoirs and other permeable geologic units.

- Initiate periodic national comprehensive carbon resource assessments of potential carbon sequestration and carbon storage vulnerability in terrestrial ecosystems and geologic formations.
- Integrate multidisciplinary methods and tools for carbon sequestration assessment and monitoring.
- Improve understanding of processes (including climate and land-use change) that control carbon storage in terrestrial (soil, sediment, vegetation, and agricultural lands), aquatic (lacustrine, fluvial, and wetland), and nearshore marine systems.
- Improve estimates of historical and present-day carbon fluxes due to water and sediment transport.
- Improve understanding of effects of elevated CO_2 concentrations on ocean acidification.

Longer term (5–10 years)

- Periodically update and refine assessments of carbon sequestration and loss from terrestrial ecosystems and geologic formations.
- Publish national maps of carbon stocks and fluxes based on integrated, multidisciplinary, multiagency studies of carbon cycling and storage.
- Contribute to international efforts to model future changes in the global carbon cycle and atmospheric CO_2 concentrations.
- Synthesize studies of ocean acidification and its impacts.

Goal 3. Improve understanding of land-use and land-cover changes: rates, causes, and consequences

Changes in land use, cover, and condition influence climate; climate and other global change factors, in turn, influence change in land use, cover, and condition. These changes alter biogeophysical, biogeochemical, and energy exchange processes, which affect weather and climate variability at local, regional, and global scales. At local and regional levels, these changes pose direct challenges for natural-resource managers as land change can fragment and degrade habitat; alter water quality and quantity; and reduce options for managing ecosystem resilience to climate change. Land-use intensification, such as irrigation, multicropping, and urban densification, must be considered due to alteration of hydrologic dynamics and nitrogen cycling, impacts on water-quality degradation, and contributions to weather and climate variability because of alteration of energy and water exchange between the land and atmosphere. Distinguishing natural variability from anthropogenic influence relies on understanding how land use, cover, and condition change. Managing land-change effects requires interdisciplinary knowledge of patterns, processes, and consequences of changes in land use and land cover to understand the interaction between human activities and natural systems over multiple spatial and temporal scales.

Because land changes have local origins and regional and global consequences, interdisciplinary land-change science investigations must focus on patterns, processes, and consequences of land-use change, land condition, and land cover at multiple spatial and temporal scales. Critical elements of this USGS Global Change science goal include:

- Monitoring patterns of land change using ground surveys and long-term, high-quality geospatial data from calibrated and validated remotely sensed imagery;
- Identifying drivers of change and applying spatially and temporally explicit models to forecast plausible scenarios of land change;

- Assessing consequences of past, present, and future land change on vulnerability and resilience of coupled human-environment systems and the services they provide; and
- Applying land-change science and knowledge to policy and decisionmaking to address consequences of land change and inform critical DOI issues.

Carrying out these elements will require close communication with organizations managing the impacts of land use, cover, and condition change, such as DOI bureaus and U.S. Department of Agriculture (USDA) agencies, State resource management agencies, and nongovernmental organizations (NGOs). Scientific partnerships with the National Aeronautics and Space Administration (NASA), NOAA, the U.S. Forest Service, the Natural Resources Conservation Service, the Bureau of Census, and others will be required to accomplish the research associated with this goal.

Vision Statement

The USGS will explain how changes in land use, cover, condition, and management alter climate, impact natural systems, and affect human health and welfare.

Major Questions

- How do climate variability and change (including extreme events) affect land use, cover, and condition?
- How has increased nitrogen from anthropogenic sources affected terrestrial and aquatic ecosystems and the services they deliver?
- How will changes in land use, cover, and condition affect the ability of ecosystems to provide essential goods and services?
- What past, current, and future patterns and attributes of land use, cover, and condition affect carbon and nitrogen cycles, sediment production, atmospheric processes, and ecosystem structure and function?
- What are the impacts of future land use, cover, and condition on sediment movement, air and water quality, water quantity, and nutrient cycles?
- What opportunities exist for managing land-use change to minimize negative impacts and maximize positive outcomes on natural and human systems?

Strategic Actions and Products

Short Term (1–5 years)

- Produce maps, statistical analyses, and reports on 5-year rates of regional and national land-use and land-cover change.
- Develop regional and national scenarios and projections of U.S. land change over 5- to 50-year periods, keyed to various economic and policy assumptions, for use in resource planning, climate, and hydrologic modeling investigations.
- Conduct sensitivity studies on how the influence of land-use and land-cover changes (LULCC) on surface albedo (reflectance), evaporation and transpiration, snow cover, greenhouse gas fluxes, and particulates affect climate; analyze how type and distribution of land cover affects regional weather and climate patterns.
- Evaluate effects of LULCC on carbon dynamics, including analyzing impacts of land use on greenhouse gas mitigation and management.

- Conduct a detailed national assessment of nitrogen deposition patterns and impacts on ecosystem structure and function, including water quality.
- Assess the impact of cumulative changes in land use, cover, and condition, in combination with climate variability and change, on the ecological integrity of the Nation's conservation lands.
- Develop decision-support tools for communication and use of land information by researchers, resource managers, and others.

Longer term (5–10 years)

- Publish maps, statistical analyses, and reports on annual rates of regional, national, and global land-use and land-cover change.
- Develop a community land-change model that couples land use, land cover, and disturbances with climate, hydrological, biogeochemical, ecosystem, and other process models.
- Report on results of how changes in land use, cover, and condition affect soils, ecosystem processes, water and nitrogen cycles, plants and wildlife changes, and the delivery of ecosystem services.
- Provide decision-support tools for communication and use of land information by researchers, resource managers, and others.

Goal 4. Improve understanding, at a process level, of changes in droughts, floods, and water availability under changing land use and climate

Water sustains human societies and ecosystems. Water in snow pack, glaciers, soils, bedrock, lakes, rivers, and streams both represents a commodity and provides a range of services but also poses risks to human populations and natural and managed ecosystems. Water affects and is affected by human activities, such as land use, water use, and fire management. Hydrological processes are key controls on human-driven changes in global cycling of carbon, nitrogen, and other elements. The water cycle and climate are inextricably linked.

Natural-resource and hazard managers, as well as emergency responders, need information and tools to confront the challenges of planning and management under highly uncertain projections of climate change. Quantifying the impacts of altered water availability on ecosystems and human societies and identifying effective management responses require climate-change information and process-based understanding. Commonly, the response of river basins to shifting climatic factors such as precipitation, radiation, and temperature are masked and may be dominated by changes in water use, water management, and land use and by natural variability at annual to multidecadal scales. These masking influences are important stressors in their own right. Projections of future precipitation amount, intensity, and event frequency have been only poorly constrained by climate science, so projections of water availability and water-related hazards are, and will continue to be, highly uncertain. Gaps in understanding of sensitivity of basin behavior to climate change increase the uncertainty. Providing managers with meaningful information for long-term planning can be accomplished by a program of research on coupled land-atmospheric processes, alongside a vigorous program of empirical research that aims to document on the basis of historical and proxy records the hydrologic changes now underway. Synthesis efforts, wherein model results and empirical water data are explored and compared on an ongoing basis, will help advance understanding.

USGS monitoring, analysis, and modeling activities can prove indispensable for detecting, understanding, and predicting changes in hydrology. The USGS led the Nation in developing monitoring methods and standards and will now lead in enhancing national monitoring systems to address global change. USGS predictive and diagnostic modeling expertise for surface water, groundwater, and water chemistry will also lead to the next generation of hydrological models. The USGS has a long history of collaboration with local, State, and national water-resources organizations, including the U.S. Bureau of Reclamation and the U.S. Army Corps of Engineers, water-resources departments in all 50 States, and hundreds of local public water agencies and institutions. Building on such collaborations will provide important baselines and many real-world opportunities to address water-resource challenges with changing water demands, including those for ecological uses and supplies, changing land use, and changing climate.

Vision Statement

The USGS will provide scientific knowledge and tools for understanding and predicting impacts of land-use and climate change on water resources. This knowledge and these tools will inform integrated resource management and adaptation strategies to ensure water for human activities and to protect human life, property, and ecosystems.

Major Questions

- How can we improve characterization of natural variability for improved management and mitigation of drought and flood impacts and to facilitate attribution of hydrologic changes to natural variability, human activities on the landscape, and decadal-centennial climate change?
- Where, when, and how do anthropogenic climate change and natural climate variability present the most urgent challenges to water-, land-, and biological-resource managers?
- Which land-use and water-use practices enhance or decrease the effects of climate change on the Nation's citizens and lands?
- How do climate change and land use impact runoff, streamflow, sediment transport, groundwater recharge, water quality, water use, and freshwater availability?
- How do climate change and land and water use affect the availability of water to terrestrial and aquatic ecosystems and thereby affect ecological patterns and processes?

Strategic Actions and Products

Short term (1–5 years)

- Define USGS national monitoring-network requirements and evaluate existing networks to facilitate timely detection of climate- and land-use-change impacts on streamflow, groundwater, and water quality.
- Re-establish monitoring at discontinued sites that already have high-quality, long-term hydrologic records needed to characterize ongoing changes.
- Accelerate analysis of long-term USGS hydrologic records with the aim to improve estimates of hydrologic statistics (for example, seasonal and annual means and extremes) and to understand their trends.
- Produce a national summary of observed and potential climate-change and land-use impacts on water availability.
- Conduct research on impacts of climate, water use, and land use on water quality to develop improved, predictive methods.
- Execute initial scoping for a national assessment of climate-change impacts on water quality.

- Assess changing sediment and dust mobilization and transport and conduct research on their relation to land use and climate.
- Produce a national-scale evaluation of changing flood and drought risks under climate change.

Longer term (5–10 years)

- Produce a national summary of observed and potential impacts of the combination of land use and climate change on water quality (in collaboration with land-use and water-quality evaluations by the USGS National Water-Quality Assessment Program).
- Produce decision-support tools for water planning and management under land-use, water-use, and climate change, including strategies, tools, and information resources for scenario-based assessments, management under uncertainty, and identification of vulnerability thresholds in resource systems.
- Produce water-use forecasts and scenarios under climate-change and land-use scenarios for planning and modeling.
- Produce national evaluation and projections of flood and drought risks under climate and land-use changes with direct ties to the National Integrated Drought Information System (NIDIS) information portals.
- Develop terrestrial-system models that synthesize understanding and predictive capabilities for hydrology, biogeochemistry, landscape conditions, biota, and ecological processes.

Goal 5. Improve understanding and prediction of coastal response to sea-level rise and climatic change

Coastal areas are highly complex systems, vulnerable to abrupt change, and stressed by human development activities. Accelerated sea-level rise, coupled with changes in storm intensity and freshwater runoff, may result in dramatic future changes in low-lying coastal systems. The relation between coastal processes and climate-related forcings has become an important focus of USGS research in recent years. Understanding onshore and nearshore impacts of global change is crucial to people who live in or are dependent on services of coastal regions. Helping coastal communities anticipate and adapt to change within defined ranges of uncertainty is now possible with tools developed and demonstrated by the USGS in its coastal studies programs and projects. These studies emphasize understanding, monitoring, and modeling of coastal processes, including impacts on threatened mangrove, coral reef, tidal marsh, and estuary and bay coastal systems.

The USGS is part of a research community that must evaluate and predict processes that cause relative sea-level change along the coast. Forecasting the rate and variability through time and along our coasts of future sea-level rise influenced by factors such as subsidence and wetland accretion depends on this research. Studies of modern processes and investigations of sea-level rise in the recent and distant past will help us understand and anticipate potential extreme and abrupt change. Research on global and regional processes, such as land subsidence due to sediment loading and groundwater extraction, regional glacio-isostatic adjustment, marsh accretion rates, vertical tectonic movements, and cryospheric mass balance and ice dynamics, is needed to assess future rates and impacts of sea-level rise. Specifically, the mass balance of the Greenland and Antarctic ice sheets, small ice caps, and alpine glaciers indicates that today's rising sea level is attributable to decreasing mass balance of land ice as well as to thermal expansion of the surface ocean. The polar amplification hypothesis holds that the rates of climate change in polar regions and high elevations of the northern hemisphere will be higher than those in temperate and tropical low-lying regions. Research on the Earth's cryosphere and its impact, seen in accelerated sea-level rise on coastal ecosystems, is necessary to predict future coastal change. Analysis of geologic and environmental records of past sea-level rise and coastal response will provide observational records to test models, identify potential for extreme change, and understand how sea-level and other environmental indicators respond to changing climate.

Vision Statement

Scientific understanding of coastal response to climate change, sea-level rise, and human development will enhance the protection of coastal resources and lead to safer, more stable coastal communities.

Major Questions

- How rapidly has sea level risen in the past? What can we expect for future relative sea-level rise over timescales ranging from years to centuries? What extremes in sea-level rise rates are possible? How does sea-level rise vary regionally?
- How will changes in seasonal storm activity and intensity affect coasts?
- How will continental shelf, slope, and coastal ecosystems, including wetlands, Arctic shorelines, coral reefs, barrier islands, and estuaries, respond to the combined impacts of storms, sea-level rise, and coastal erosion?
- How will the combination of changing storm conditions, sea-level rise, and changes in wetlands, coral reefs, and barrier islands impact the vulnerability and resiliency of coastal communities, fisheries, tourism, and other economic and ecosystems services?
- How will low-lying coastal systems along the U.S. coastline respond to sea-level rise with and without adaptation measures?
- How will sea-level rise and climate change affect small islands and Interior trust territories in the Pacific and Atlantic regions?

Strategic Actions and Products

Short term (1–5 years)

- Process-oriented studies to quantitatively identify impacts of sea-level rise and other stressors on coastal systems for each U.S. coastal region.
- Sea-level studies to reduce gaps in current knowledge and uncertainty about potential responses of coasts, estuaries, wetlands, and human populations to sea-level rise.
- High-resolution sea-level rise scenarios for U.S. coastlines, in cooperation with partners like NOAA and appropriate USGS field-led partnerships, incorporating coastal, eustatic, and steric processes.
- Predictive models of coastal retreat, land-use and habitat change, and land loss under a range of sea-level rise and concomitant coastal protection scenarios.
- Synthesis of current science regarding likely and maximum rates of sea-level rise, combining cryospheric, geologic, biologic, hydrologic, remote-sensing, and modeling assets of the USGS.
- Synthesis of information on glacier mass balance in the United States and, in collaboration with outside organizations, synthesis of glacier and ice-sheet contributions to sea-level rise.

Longer term (5–10 years)

- Watershed and coastal integrated impact studies of changing freshwater discharge, sediment, and nutrient influx on coastal receiving waters.

- National coastline monitoring and mapping of physical and environmental changes using new geospatial technologies and high-resolution elevation data to produce a national coastline vulnerability assessment.
- Reconstructions from the historic and geologic records of sea level to provide important baseline conditions for periods of warm climate and elevated greenhouse gas concentrations.
- Assessments of sea-level rise and climate change for U.S. islands and insular territories.
- Assessments of changing coastal vulnerability as a consequence of climate-change- driven alterations of protective natural features (wetlands, coral reefs, barrier beaches, and Arctic sea ice).
- Datasets on coastal inundation by storm surge for use in coastal hydrodynamic modeling to assess storm-surge risk and future sea-level rise.

Goal 6. Improve understanding and prediction of biological responses to global change

Current projections for the coming decades point to rapid alterations of climate; land cover, use, and condition; and physical and chemical conditions that will pose significant challenges to managing our ecosystems and biological resources. Loss and fragmentation of habitat via climate change or land use; modification of freshwater resources; changes in wildfire frequency and impacts, insect outbreaks, and other disturbance regimes; and zoonotic diseases spread by humans are among the drivers that threaten the viability and genetic diversity of populations and communities.

It is anticipated that biota will generally shift to higher latitudes and altitudes as the climate warms, although there may be unexpected responses as these changes cross tipping points for ecosystems, populations, and species. In addition, the scope and rate of biotic responses to rising temperatures will be affected by shifts in precipitation regimes, availability of suitable substrates and habitats, and other environmental factors. Changes in seasonality will influence both plant and animal phenology, potentially disrupting crucial interactions that influence species persistence as well as how ecosystems function and what services they provide. In some cases, new connections among habitats and unintentional dispersal by humans will provide new opportunities for organisms to spread, sometimes between continents. , These conditions can lead to new problems when climate change, coupled with this new mobility, allows pests, pathogens, and invasive species to colonize habitats from which they were previously excluded. Many biotic changes are already underway, giving national urgency to addressing these challenges.

The USGS will provide the science needed to support the management of biological resources in this rapidly changing world. Our studies of past climatic and environmental changes provide insights into how life on our planet reacts to large-scale changes in climate and atmospheric chemistry. Extensive long-term monitoring efforts allow the USGS to determine how species and ecosystems are responding to climatic and land-use changes. Efforts such as the National Phenology Network, the Climate Effects Network, the National Climate Change and Wildlife Science Center (NCCWSC), and the regional Climate Science Centers (CSCs) should expand our capabilities to assess issues, such as:
- Species and ecosystem threshold response to change.
- Potential future impacts of climate and land-use change on ecological services.
- Possible effects of climate and land-use change on genetic diversity.
- Temporal rates and spatial extents of biological impacts.

Attention will focus on identifying regions and ecosystems especially vulnerable to the effects of changes in climate, land use, and other environmental factors, in concert with appropriate partners. Interior Bureaus, State natural resources and conservations agencies, and NGOs should be included.

Vision statement

The USGS will provide scientific knowledge needed to manage the Nation's biological endowment affected by rapidly changing climate and land use. This knowledge will form the scientific basis for wise administration of vulnerable and critical ecosystems, wildlife resources and their habitats, and managed lands.

Major Questions

- How will changes in climate and land use, cover, and condition influence regional ecosystem structure and function, and how will these ecosystem changes feed back to climate, hydrology, and biogeochemical cycles?
- How will ecological response be influenced by the spatial and temporal scales at which climate varies and changes?
- How will species and ecosystems respond to global change? Will their vulnerabilities and response thresholds to global change be altered by changes in atmospheric chemistry, loss of genetic diversity, and other factors?
- How will global change affect biodiversity from genetic to population scales across ecosystems?
- How will changes in climate and land use, cover, and condition affect the distribution and extent of current and potential habitats that host ecosystems, populations, and species?
- How will habitat fragmentation and changes in connections among habitats affect the ability of species and ecosystems to adjust their geographic distributions in response to global change?
- How will other critical ecological stressors (invasive species, pathogens, and insect outbreaks) interact with climate change to affect ecosystem components and processes? How might their mitigation help curb the ecological impacts of climate change?

Strategic Actions and Products

Short term (1–5 years)

- Investigate how biological systems have adapted to past changes in climate, land use, and atmospheric chemistry.
- Integrate data from State and Federal entities and NGOs to create dynamic, nationally integrated maps of the distribution of species and their habitats, linked to other information needed for science and management.
- Work with other agencies and the broader scientific community to establish standards, priorities, and networks to better monitor ongoing changes in species, ecosystems, and landscapes as influenced by abiotic and biotic factors.
- Develop knowledge and expertise to identify key processes and response thresholds in biological responses to global change across terrestrial and aquatic habitats.
- Develop regional science agendas in collaboration with resource managers and scientific experts; use these regional agendas to identify commonalities and issues deserving national scale action.
- Identify ecosystems most vulnerable to global change and develop research and monitoring strategies for these areas that include documenting their biodiversity and baseline conditions of processes and biota.
- Map current and likely future habitat fragmentation and connectivity in targeted landscapes.

- Document genetic diversity for plant and wildlife species of concern and biodiversity in ecosystems of concern.
- Conduct ecosystem-scale studies of ecosystem thresholds based on model-predicted future climate-change scenarios and paleoecological reconstructions of ecosystem history.
- Develop an integrated process model that combines landscape properties; land use, cover, and condition; and disturbances with climate, hydrological, biogeochemical, ecosystem, and other process models to predict impacts of future changes.

Monitoring: A Critical Component of Global Change Science and Adaptive Resource Management

A strong, relevant, and integrated monitoring program is a foundation of global change science and, therefore, the USGS Climate and Land Use Change Mission Area. Monitoring factors of environmental change and their effects on natural resources is a high priority for the Interior Bureaus and other resource-management partners at the State and Federal levels. Meeting current and future challenges in monitoring and detecting an expanded range of environmental variables will require the USGS to upgrade, improve, and, in some cases, reposition its current networks. Iinnovative approaches and new perspectives can be employed to address an expanded range of environmental variables. Effective partnerships with other institutions monitoring global change and its impacts on natural resources will maximize efficiencies by jointly planning and implementing monitoring strategies.

The USGS Science Strategy (2007) recognized the central role of monitoring, recommending that global change research should rely on existing "decades of observational data and long-term records to interpret consequences of climate variability and change to the Nation's biological populations, ecosystems, and land and water resources."

Examples of monitoring needed to address in section "Science Goals and Objectives" are:
- Detection of changes and trends in shorelines in response to sea-level rise, subsidence, storms, and human development; trends in accretion rates; and other processes that affect sustainability of coastal systems.
- Timing, amounts, and availability of water; impacts of droughts and floods on terrestrial and aquatic resources.
- Rates and geographic extent of land-use and land-cover change.
- Effects of human activities on landscape properties and on carbon cycling; carbon storage in soils and plants; biological response to increased atmospheric CO_2 concentrations.
- Changes in abundance and distribution of plants and animals; trends in variables that indicate ecosystem condition.

The necessity to monitor interdependencies among global change drivers and their effects highlights the need for an integrated, Bureau-level monitoring emphasis and strategy.

Throughout its history, the USGS has been a national and international leader in the conception, design, and implementation of cooperative monitoring networks to track environmental indicators. USGS remote-sensing capabilities, for example, provide more than 40 years of evidence of global changes in the Earth's land and water, while USGS hydrologic monitoring networks provide data stretching back, in some locations, to the late 19th Century. USGS monitoring capabilities include nationwide monitoring of hydrology, land cover and use, migratory birds, species-through-ecosystem conditions, and phenology. USGS monitoring platforms range from detailed process measurements at plot scales, to widely distributed streamgage networks, light detection and ranging (LiDAR), and other specialized tools, such as airborne and satellite imaging systems.

Many current monitoring protocols and networks were designed with other data needs in mind and may not be capable of detecting and tracking the gradual changes anticipated in response to climate-driven global-level change trends. First, priorities for monitoring locations may change. USGS streamgages monitor many locations that are important to flood prediction and reservoir management and are commonly funded on a cooperative basis but may lack the ability to monitor areas sensitive to global change. The monitoring of plant or animal populations designed to detect the effects of one threat may need to be changed to address new issues. Second, global change effects may require significant increases in monitoring for emerging issues, such as dust, nitrogen deposition, and carbon and sediment transport in rivers. Third, it will be increasingly important to establish multivariable monitoring networks, where hydrologic, biotic, meteorologic, and other factors are measured at the same locations. Placement of sites needs to be planned such that these in-situ measurements can be "scaled up" to a larger geographic context to provide comprehensive monitoring of plants, animals, and ecosystem condition and to detect land changes in areas that lack in-situ monitoring. Synoptic monitoring of selected geo- and biophysical variables using remote sensing is an important tool in scaling up plot data and, therefore, in assessing how human and natural disturbances affect physical landscapes, plants, animals, and ecosystem condition. With its rich historical land remote-sensing archive, the USGS can provide the consistent, calibrated terrestrial time-series datasets needed to detect and monitor global change events and processes. However, as with other monitoring activities, land remote-sensing systems will need to be managed specifically to detect and understand biotic and abiotic conditions and trends attributable to global change.

The USGS can lead evaluation and design of new multipurpose, multivariable monitoring networks even as it continues quantitative enhancements of existing monitoring systems to assure data for timely, reliable, and authoritative detection and attribution of global change impacts.

Monitoring at multiple spatial and temporal scales with locally to nationally consistent measurements and integrated data products will require coordination among the Climate and Land Use Change Mission Area, other USGS programs and mission areas, and our external partners engaged in monitoring (for example, States, NOAA, NASA, the NSF, the U.S. Army Corps of Engineers, the Bureau of Land Management, and the National Park Service). Coordination will strengthen each organization's efforts, help develop common protocols, allow better interoperability among databases, and effectively communicate results to all, including policymakers and the public.

Strategic Actions and Products

Three specific actions will help guide the USGS Climate and Land Use Change Mission Area in designing and instituting an integrated and strategic monitoring plan:

1. Establish a standing USGS Monitoring Advisory Group, comprised of representatives from USGS science centers and national-level programs, to determine what global change monitoring efforts are best suited for USGS by:

   - Identifying core USGS monitoring strengths.
   - Expanding and confirming future monitoring needs outlined in this report.
   - Identifying gaps where USGS core monitoring capabilities could be applied.
   - Identifying and recommending research needed to support monitoring efforts.
   - Recommending ways to modify current monitoring efforts to better detect global change and the protocol development needed to enhance detection of global change.

- Recommending ways to fill the voids in monitoring that hamper progress toward the goals described in Section 3.

2. Work with partners to establish a standing Interagency Monitoring Advisory Group comprised of representatives from the USGS Monitoring Advisory Group (above) and external partners to develop a clear monitoring strategy spanning site-specific to global scales. This monitoring strategy will minimize duplication of effort and maximize coverage, integration, reliability, and timeliness of global change detection through partnerships. The group is needed to address the following key questions:

    - What data are needed at what scales for accurate detection of long-term change?
    - Are current observational and monitoring networks adequate for detecting changes associated with global change in a timely and reliable manner?
    - How can partnerships enhance existing and planned networks, what will be the governance for these partnerships, and who would be responsible for what data?
    - What new methods, standards, sites, and observations need to be developed and integrated to provide the monitoring necessary for change detection, attribution of causes of change, and management of consequences?
    - How can new data, previously collected information, and data from different observational methods and different agencies be integrated in a manner most useful to scientists, managers, policymakers, and the public?
    - How do we monitor opportunistically after extreme climatic events and ecological disturbances, such as in evaluating pathways of succession after episodes of fires, insect outbreaks, and plant die-offs synchronized at the regional to subcontinental scale (for example, the 2002–2003 drought in the American West)?
    - How can remotely sensed and in-situ data be most effectively integrated to develop consistent time series useful for detecting and monitoring evidence of global change?
    - How can data from the geologic record, historical data, and newly collected data be used to assess the efficacy of models that simulate observed environmental responses to climate change and land use? How can information from these data-model comparisons be used to improve our ability to project potential future changes in plants, animals, and water resources?
    - How can long-term or spatially extensive datasets be used for detection of global change? For example, how can migratory bird information or historical photos and images for change-detection maps of critical and sensitive areas be used to detect global change?

3. Enhance and ensure effective USGS monitoring of global change phenomena through:

    A. Manage national land remote-sensing assets; implement, in conjunction with NASA, the Landsat Data Continuity Mission (Landsat 8) and future Landsat missions; develop calibrated and validated geophysical measurements and integrated data products with accuracy and precision needed to map, measure, and monitor land changes attributed to climate change, other natural disturbances, and human activity; and identify and evaluate new remote-sensing technologies to provide measurements needed to detect and monitor global change.

    B. Use recommendations from the advisory groups above to establish monitoring sites in areas highly vulnerable to global change. Multiple variables (hydrologic, climatic, biotic

processes and components, socioeconomic, and other factors) will be measured at these sites in ways that allow these groups to answer local-to-national scale questions.
 C. Maintain and enhance more specialized networks (for example, stream gages, dust sources, deposition, and animal populations) where needed to detect global change.

Communicating Science to Society—Services, Products, and Delivery

Recognition by policymakers, resource managers, and the public of the increasing pace and unpredictability of global change is generating increased demand for information about the nature of impending changes and how to respond to them effectively. There is also consensus, within USGS and elsewhere, that the nature of projected future environmental change will require expanded and better integrated scientific and observational activities and that those adaptation strategies will be enhanced by landscape- and regional-level partnerships of science and management.

USGS scientists will meet the needs of our changing world by providing timely, scientifically sound, state-of-the-science information on global change and its effects in a variety of formats and venues. USGS science is used by a wide range of people and institutions, from highly technical, global-scale scientific collaborations to individuals seeking information on river stages for recreational boating. The Bureau delivers its science in multiple forms, which include Web-enabled databases, peer-reviewed literature, and technical assistance to resource managers. The portfolio of scientific activities described in this strategic plan will complement the work of a large array of international, Federal, State, tribal, NGO, academic, and private partners.

Services and Products

Research Results—From Fundamental to Applied

USGS Global Change research consists of investigating the fundamental biological, hydrological, geological, chemical, and physical processes that underlie global stressors and environmental response. Results of these scientific investigations will serve as the building blocks for additional scientific progress and can be applied to a variety of outputs and tools.
 A. *Research Findings:* USGS scientists, as active members of a global scientific community, will continue to contribute to the growth of scientific knowledge about how the Earth system functions. In addition to providing building blocks for additional scientific progress, many research results are used by managers directly, often with significant assistance, advice, and collaboration from USGS scientists. This direct and hands-on interaction is often crucial to effective transfer and application of research findings.
 B. *Assessments:* Assessments provide scientific synthesis and analysis of patterns, trends, pace, and global, national, regional, and sectorial issues affecting Earth systems. They provide key findings, new understanding, strategies, and new or improved methods that can assist and guide policymakers and resource managers in monitoring, mitigation, and adaptation decisions linked to global change and in providing information to the public. Assessments by the USGS and its partners will use existing and new observations to detect and describe effects of global change on natural resources, environmental conditions, and people.
 C. *Methods and Tools:* Standard methods and tested tools provided by the USGS to further the standard for scientific and management knowledge. Among these products are dynamic, mechanistic, statistical, conceptual, and other types of models that portray how global systems behave at multiple temporal and spatial scales; the likelihood and consequences of actions,

drivers, interrelationships, trends, and forecasts; and consequences of adaption and mitigation techniques. Also included are basic research field and laboratory techniques, monitoring-program designs, and data-integration methods.

Modeling and Projection

Understanding how natural systems function and observing their past and present behavior form a powerful intellectual basis for making informed statements about the future. USGS scientists develop and participate in a wide range of modeling efforts, from projections of flows, particularly streams under changed climatic conditions, to tackling crucial elements of global models used by the IPCC.

These models continue to evolve as fundamental knowledge of natural systems grows through expanded research and observation and as modeling techniques are refined. The USGS will work to enhance and evolve USGS modeling to reduce uncertainty through consistent modeling approaches; integration and linking hydrologic, geological, land-use, and ecological projections of change; and expanding access to resulting data.

Technical Support

A goal of USGS global change science is to translate and deliver scientific results of maximum value to other scientists and natural resource managers. Transferring scientific knowledge for application to real-world problems is facilitated by direct interaction between scientists and resource managers or decisionmakers. The USGS will continue to strengthen this capability by encouraging interaction among individual scientists (including consideration within both the Research Grade Evaluation and the Equipment and Development Grade Evaluation criteria). USGS programs and stakeholders, including resource managers and the public. USGS will use these interactions to develop decision support tools to help communicate with stakeholders within an adaptive management framework. This nexus between science and management will ensure that USGS science programs respond to management needs and that resulting science products are accessible, appropriately translated, and effectively applied.

Enabling Efficient Transformation of Data to Knowledge

The USGS has a unique legacy as the producer of long-term datasets for multiple uses, many of which are geographically extensive. Complex scientific questions posed by global change and its impact on Earth systems require analysis, integration, synthesis, and modeling of science data and information from multiple disciplines, locations, and timescales. Complex data, models, and other information from a variety of sources, in different formats, spatial scales, and resolutions, will need to be integrated and made available for policymakers, resource managers, and partners and for public use. A comprehensive global change informatics strategy for data and infrastructure will enable scientists, partners, and stakeholders to create, disseminate, find, access, and use new and existing global change data from the USGS and other sources.

Delivering Science—USGS Framework for Collaboration and Communication

The USGS recognizes that if science is to be responsive to societal needs, we must communicate effectively with those who use the products of our global change science program. USGS will take advantage its national presence to expand communication and collaboration. This plan supports a coordinated multiagency (Federal, State, tribal, and local) national strategy that renews and expands communication and collaboration efforts that will integrate climate and land use and efficient use of resources.

The USGS was authorized under P.L. 110-161 (2008) to establish a National Climate Change and Wildlife Science Center (NCCWSC) as well as regional centers. The USGS NCCWSC, in collaboration with DOI Climate Science Centers, Landscape Conservation Cooperatives, and NGOs, will jointly design and implement research and monitoring activities, and technical support and translation of research results for application in a management context and in a manner that directly supports societal understanding and adaptation to global change. The NCCWSC will be the strategic source for USGS Global Change collaboration and communication effort, engaging partners at the national, State, regional, and local levels.

National: The framework for collaboration among U.S. Federal agencies is the U.S. Global Change Research Program (USGCRP). The USGCRP Office and its interagency working groups (IWGs) each provide vehicles for communicating and promulgating USGCRP science. The USGS will consider expanding its involvement and representation on these IWGs as an effective way to integrate USGS science and science planning with others, to ensure that high-priority issues for the USGS and its partners are reflected in the national agenda for adaptation science, and to increase visibility for USGS science.

Regional: The USGS recognizes that increased collaboration at a landscape and regional scale is needed to address global change. The USGS is helping establish eight regional Climate Science Centers (CSCs, fig. 5) as part of a larger Interior-wide climate partnership initiative that also includes Landscape Conservation Cooperatives (LCCs, fig. 6), which function as management-science interfaces involving State and Federal partners. The new CSCs will provide scientific information, tools, and techniques that land, water, wildlife, and cultural resource managers can apply to anticipate, monitor, and adapt to climate change. LCC steering committees will include representatives from governmental entities (Federal, State, tribal, and local), as well as NGOs that are prepared to contribute to the joint effort.

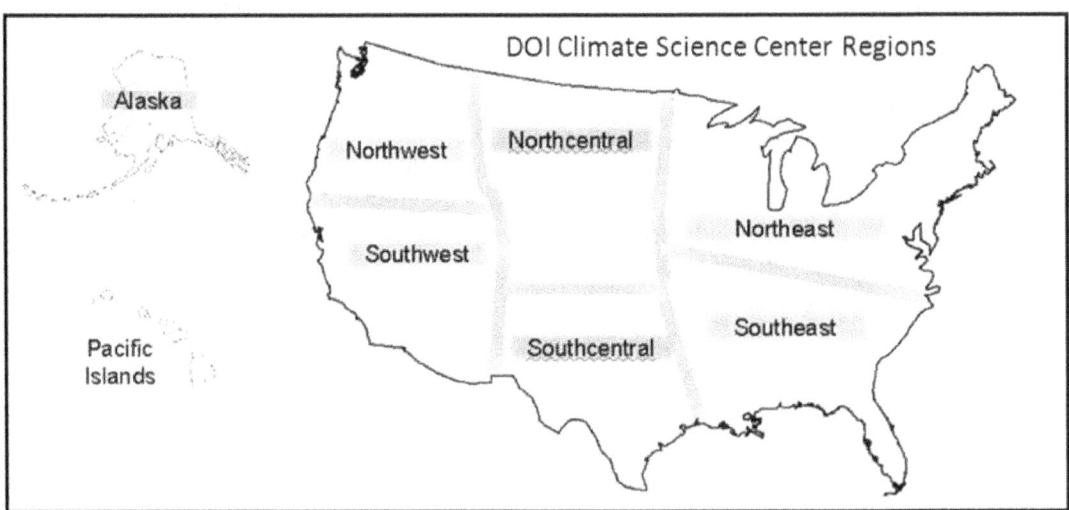

Figure 5.   Approximate working boundaries of the eight DOI Climate Science Centers.

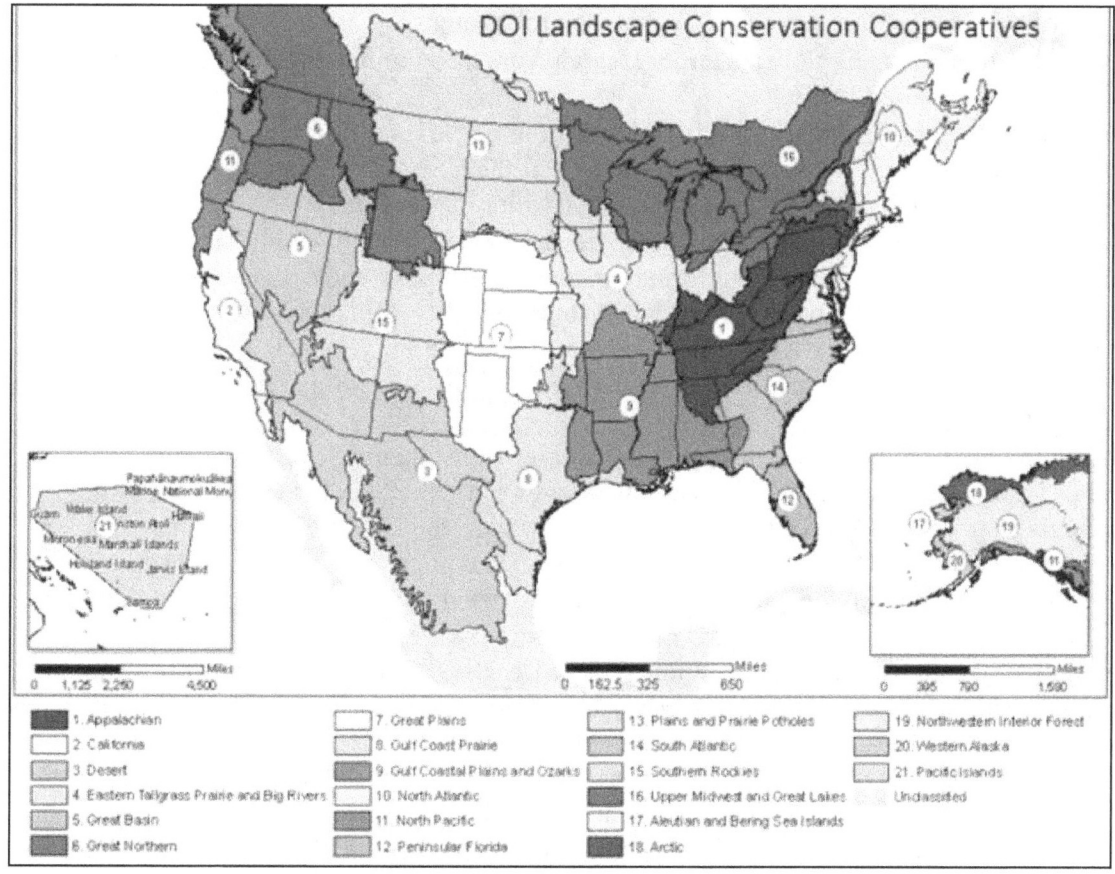

Figure 6. Map depicting the boundaries of the 21 Landscape Conservation Cooperatives. (Source: U.S. Fish and Wildlife Service)

State and Local: States are partners in the full range of USGS scientific products, and demand for these products is increasing as States expand their efforts to adapt to a variety of land and ecosystem changes. States have major management responsibilities that will be affected by global change, and they devote significant management and science resources to these issues. Local governments, tribes, and private resource managers are also expanding their efforts to address these changes and, in doing so, are looking to the USGS for critical information. Interactions with these partners involve identifying management concerns, jointly designing and implementing research and monitoring activities, and providing technical support and translation of research results for application in a management context. The USGS will work closely with resource-management agencies through the CSCs and LCCs to integrate science efforts in support of State and local science needs.

Communication: Poor communication is a serious obstacle to productivity, coordination, and effective planning in any shared endeavor. Improved internal communication was cited as a high priority by USGS scientists at the 2006 and 2010 USGS Global Change Science Workshops. Providing opportunities for linking our scientists and keeping them apprised of program developments, opportunities, and science planning were also cited as a need by field scientists and by participants from USGS regional offices and other DOI bureau representatives at both workshops. Improving internal communications should be a top priority for the Global Change program in FY2011 and beyond.

The USGS Global Change Program should initiate the following:

- Regular national USGS global change research workshops to integrate efforts and information flow throughout the Bureau.
- Internal self-subscribed mailing lists and Web sites at the level of major global change programs, each of the science goals in section 3, and each of the USGCRP IWGs, as well as at the broad disciplinary and interdisciplinary collaborative levels.
- An integrated global change information gateway for collaboration and seamless access to projects, resulting data, models, information, decision-support tools, derived products, that highlight services of the program and increase its visibility, effectiveness, and transparency. This activity will likely require support of a full-time person in the Global Change Program Office to meet internal communication needs and must be coordinated closely with the new Informatics and Data Integration Mission Area.

In addition to improving internal communications, the Strategic Science Planning Team recommends improving external communications through the USGS Global Change Web site. As part of the home page, in coordination with other Federal agencies, the USGS could develop a public outreach initiative specifically to translate and communicate complexities of global change research in a clear and consistent manner to the American public in order to highlight implications of this research to human and ecological landscapes. Success of such an initiative would improve the public's understanding of global-change-research findings. The USGS Office of Communications should continue to support the program through its contacts with the news media, press releases, social media, public presentations, and Congressional hearings and presentations.

> **Action:** A small committee of USGS global change scientists and communications experts should be formed to develop an internal and external communications strategy. This group should develop a short-range (FY11) plan for upgrading the USGS Global Change Web site and consider the initiative concept above. The team should also identify actions that would improve communications about program developments among USGS managers and scientists, such as internal newsletters or Intranet postings, periodic workshops for scientists, and Webinars.

Summary—Understanding and Responding to Climate and Land-Use Change

Natural processes, in combination with the effects of human actions, can result in global changes with large potential consequences for the natural world and society. Uncertainty about these changes and their consequences limits the Nation's ability to respond appropriately, and policymakers, resource managers, and the public are increasingly demanding more and better information to support mitigation and adaptation efforts. As the only integrated natural resources research organization in the Federal Government, the USGS plays a critical role in providing the global-change information that will help the economy, the environment, and human communities remain strong. For example, USGS assessments are providing a scientific basis for development of carbon-sequestration and energy strategies aimed at minimizing the negative effects of future climate changes.

By achieving the visions and goals presented in this science strategy, **the USGS can become the Nation's leader and gateway for accessing information and understanding past, present, and future effects of climate and land-use change on natural resources and human communities**. The USGS Global Change Program will allow policymakers and resource managers make difficult decisions regarding the management and stewardship of lands, resources, and communities. This strategy emphasizes the importance of a coordinated intra- and multiagency (Federal, State, and local) national strategy that renews and expands communication and collaboration efforts with stakeholders and partners.

When implemented, this plan will accomplish the following:

1. Build on USGS leadership in global change.
2. Fill gaps in our knowledge of how the natural and human-altered world is changing.
3. Extend strategic partnerships.
4. Improve communication and collaboration.
5. Ensure a sustained observational effort.
6. Address topics critical for managing natural resources and the environment, with tangible effects on environmental goods, services, and risks.
7. Use USGS core capacity, disciplinary strengths, integrative capacities, and long-term databases.
8. Invest in comprehensive, integrated observation and monitoring to understand local to global change processes and conditions.

References Cited

IPCC, 2007, Climate change impacts, adaptations and vulnerability: Intergovernmental Panel on Climate Change, Working Group 2, Fourth Assessment Report, Cambridge University Press, London, UK, 976 p.

McNutt, M.K., 2010, Global change strategic science planning and high-level budget development; charge to Science Strategy Planning Team (SSPT): Director's memorandum to USGS staff, January 26, 2010.

National Research Council (NRC), 1999, Global environmental change; research pathways for the next decade: National Academy Press, Washington, D.C., 603 p.

NRC, 2009, Informing decisions in a changing climate: Panel on strategies and methods for climate-related decision support, National Academies Press, Washington, D.C., 188 p.

Salazar, Ken, 2009, Department of the Interior, Secretarial Order 3289, Subject: Addressing the impacts of climate change on America's water, land and other natural and cultural resources: September 14, 2009.

Sarmiento, J.L., and Wofsy, S.C., 1999, A U.S. carbon cycle science plan; report of the Carbon and Climate Working Group for the U.S. Global Change Research Program: Washington, D.C.: U.S. Global Change Research Program.

U.S. Congress, 1990, U.S. Global Change Research Act of 1990: Public Law 101-606 (11/16/90) 104 Stat. 3096-3104. Available online at *http://www.gcrio.org/gcact1990.shtml*.

USGCRP, 2009, Global climate change impacts in the United States: U.S. Global Change Research Program, Washington, D.C., 189 p.

USGCRP, 2010, Our changing planet; the U.S. Climate Change Science Program for fiscal year 2010: U.S. Global Change Research Program, Washington, D.C., 172 p.

USGCRP, in press, Our changing planet; The U.S. Climate Change Science Program for fiscal year 2011: U.S. Global Change Research Program, Washington, D.C.

USGS, 2007, Facing tomorrow's challenges—U.S. Geological Survey science in the decade 2007–2017: U.S. Geological Survey Circular 1309, Reston, Va., 69 p. Available online at *http://pubs.usgs.gov/circ/2007/1309/.*

USGS, 2009, National Climate Change and Wildlife Science Center; proposed 5-year strategy (2009–2014): U.S. Geological Survey, Reston, Va., 21 p.

USGS, 2010, USGS Science planning, funding, and implementation model: USGS internal document prepared by the Regional Executives and Chief Scientists Team, U.S. Geological Survey, Reston, Va.

USGS, 2010, Aligning USGS senior leadership structure with the USGS Science Strategy: U.S. Geological Survey Fact Sheet 2010–3066, 4 p. Available online at *http://pubs.usgs.gov/fs/2010/3066.*

USGS, 2011, Budget justifications and performance information fiscal Year 2011: U.S. Geological Survey, Reston, Va.